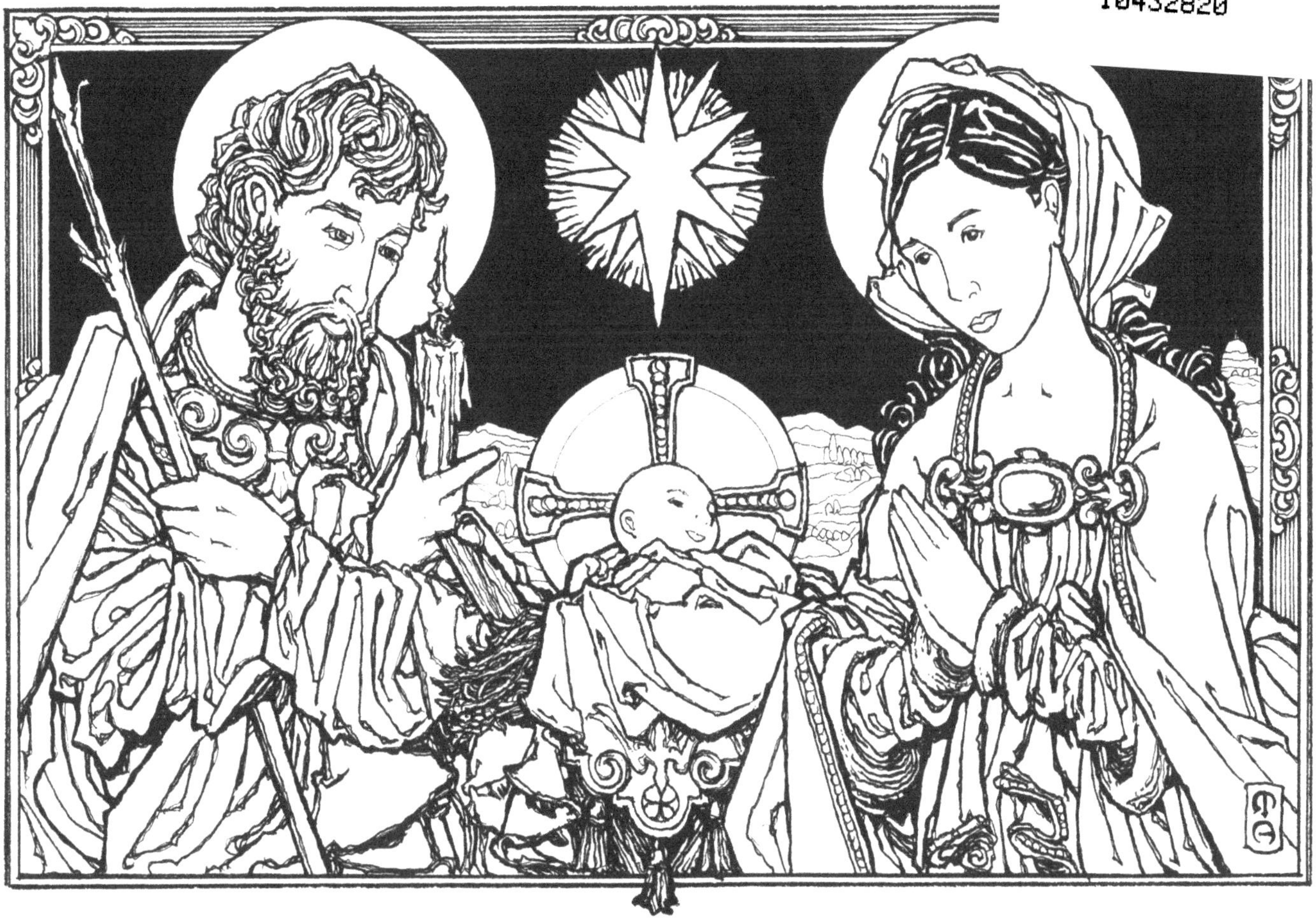

Feasts of Our Lord and Our Lady

Matthew Alderman

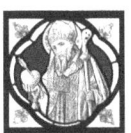

2016

ST. AUGUSTINE ACADEMY PRESS

HOMER GLEN, ILLINOIS

Copyright ©2016 by St. Augustine Academy Press

All illustrations ©2016 by Matthew Alderman. Used with permission.
Book Design by Lisa Bergman.

All Rights Reserved.

No part of this book may be reproduced or transmitted in any form or by any
electronic or mechanical means, including photocopying, recording
or by any information storage and retrieval systems,
without permission in writing from Matthew Alderman.

Published in 2016
by St. Augustine Academy Press,
Homer Glen, Illinois.

ISBN 978-1-936639-78-6

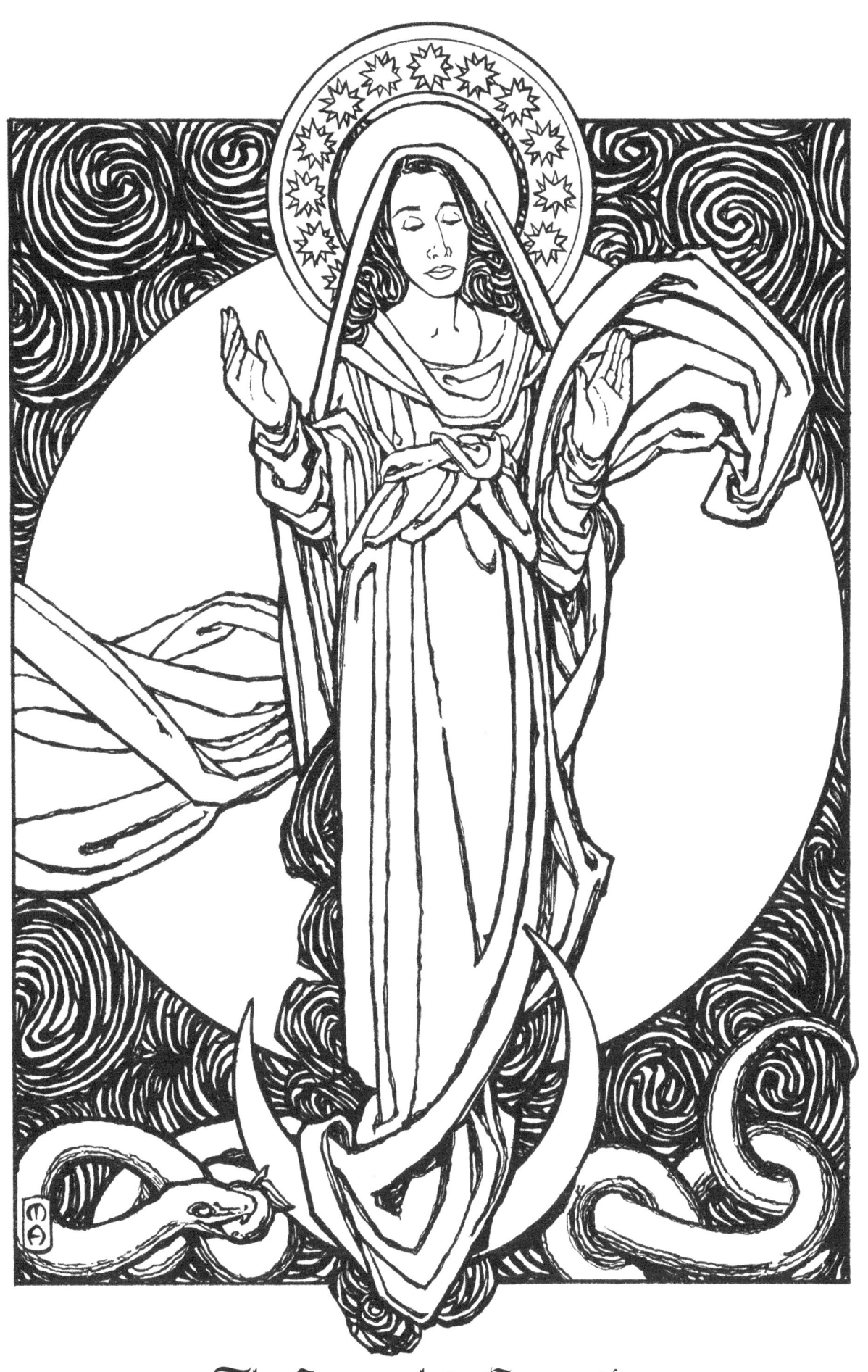

The Immaculate Conception

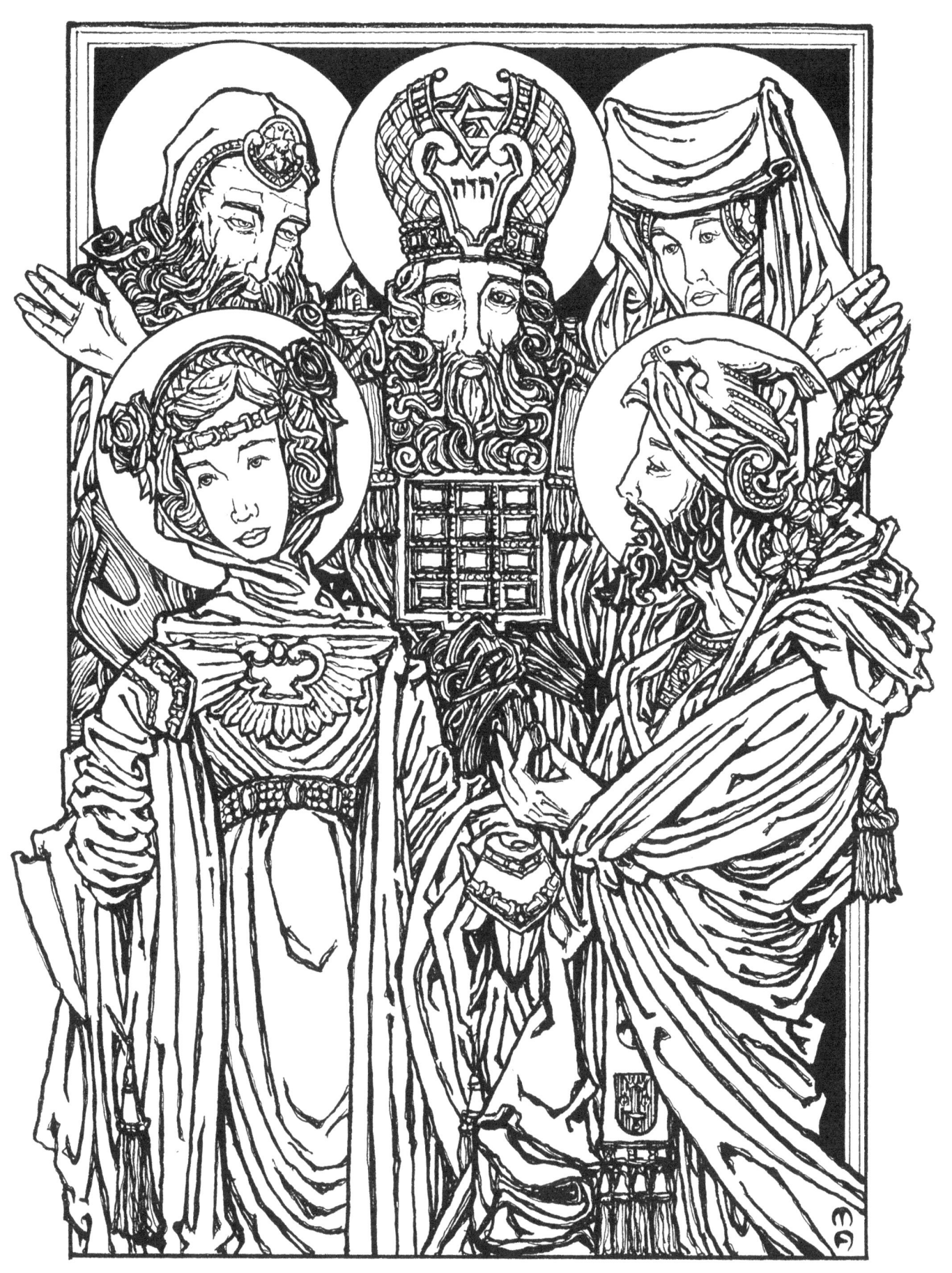

The Espousal of the Virgin

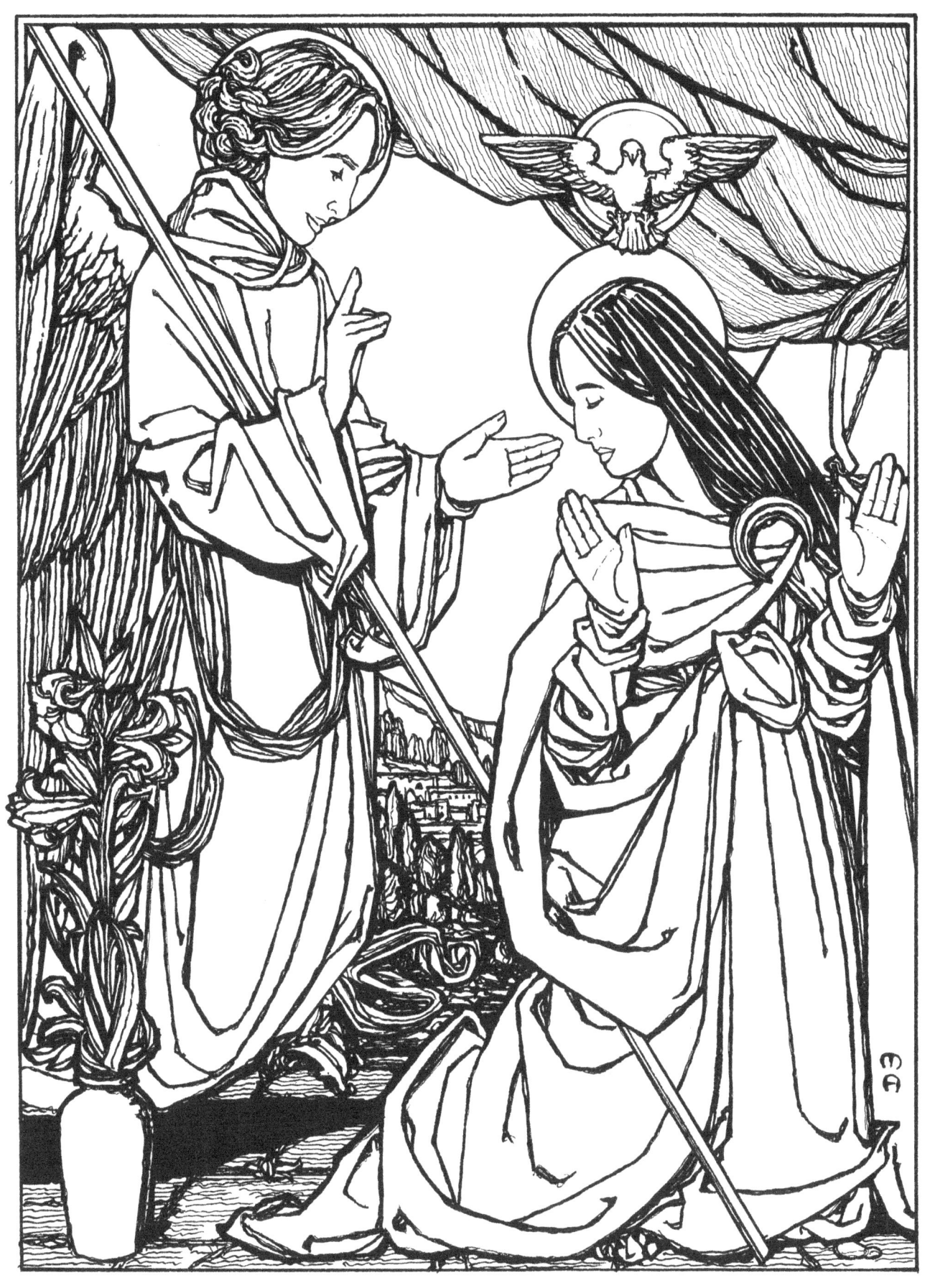

The Annunciation

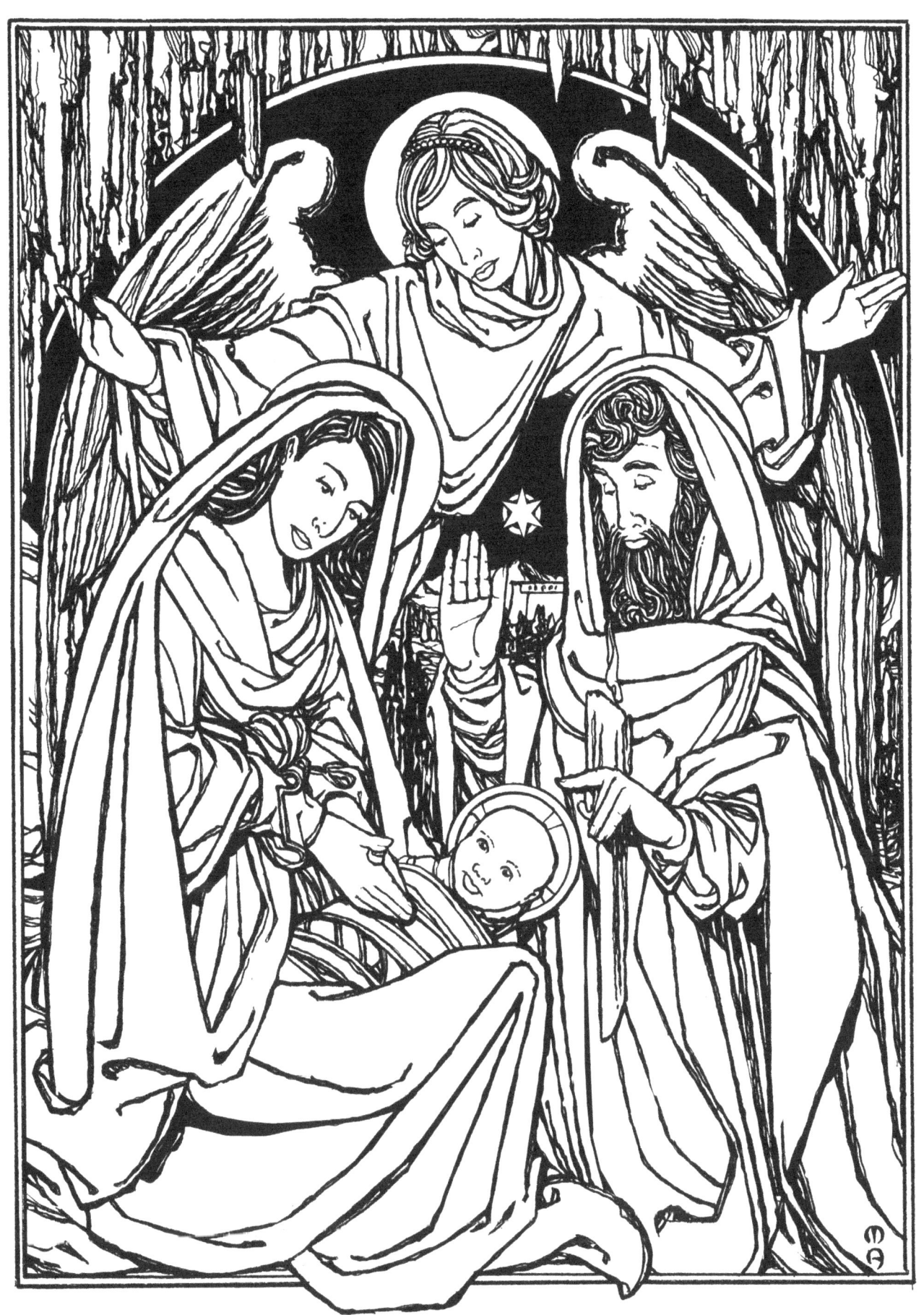

The Nativity

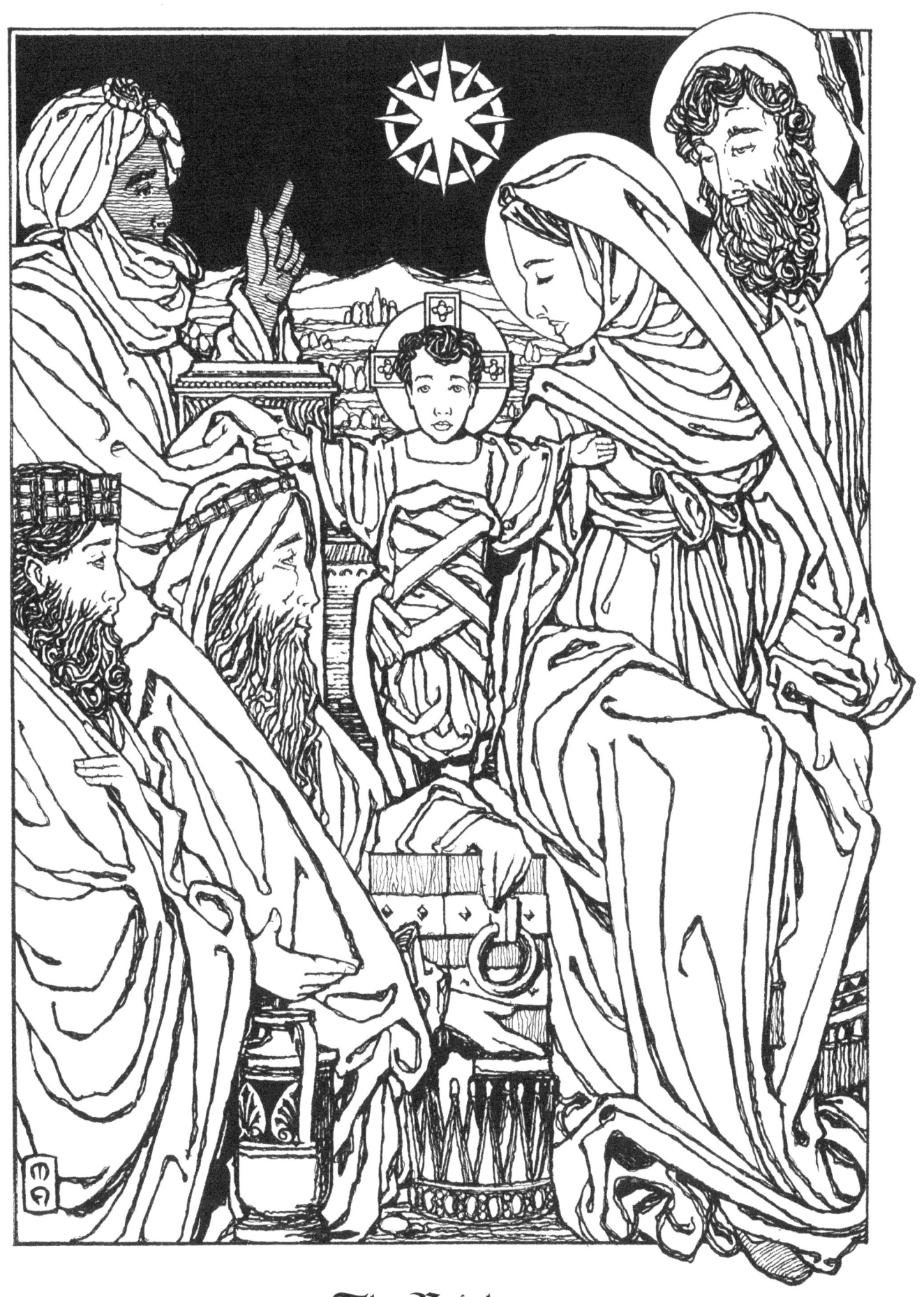

The Epiphany

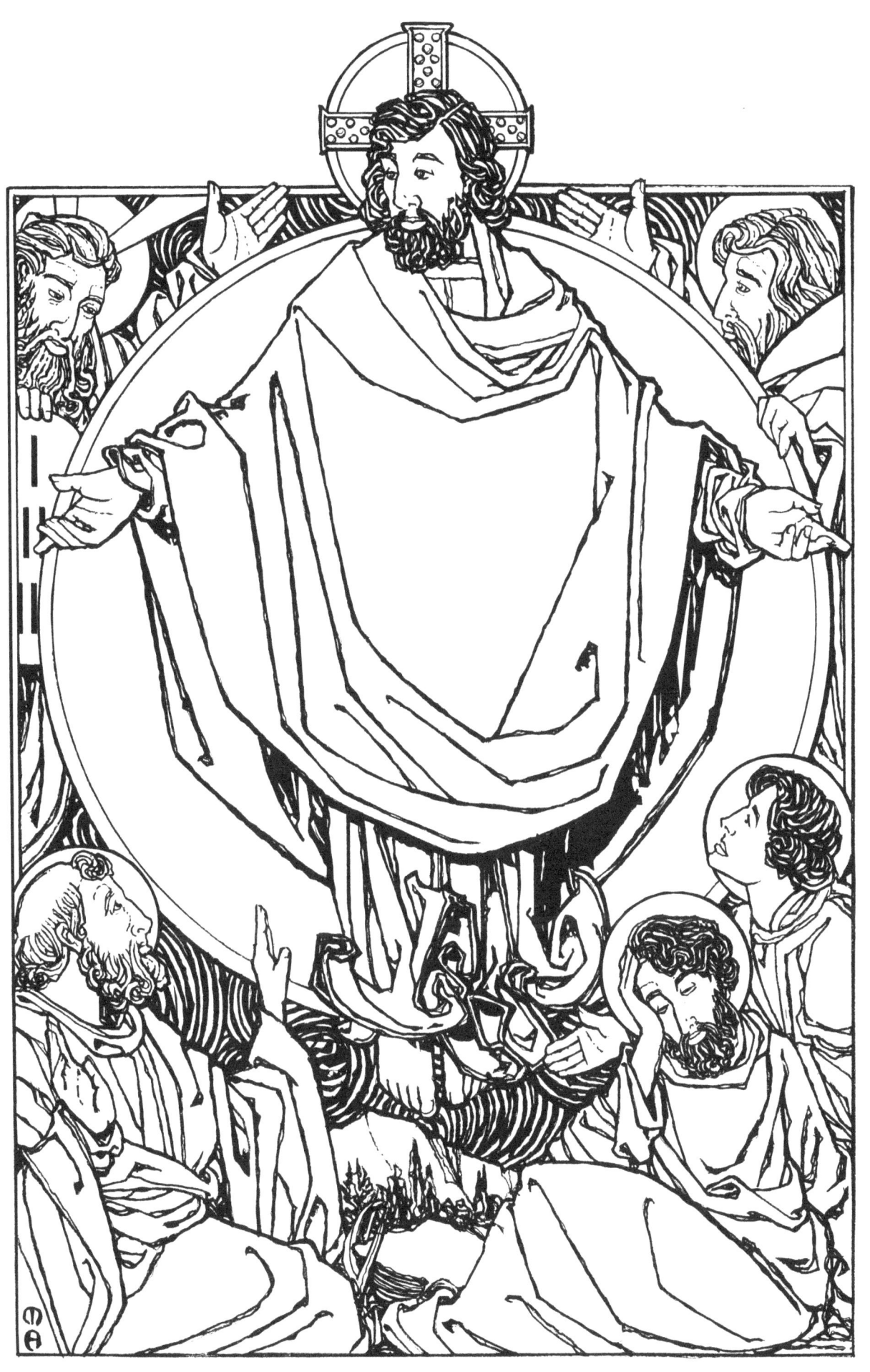

The Transfiguration

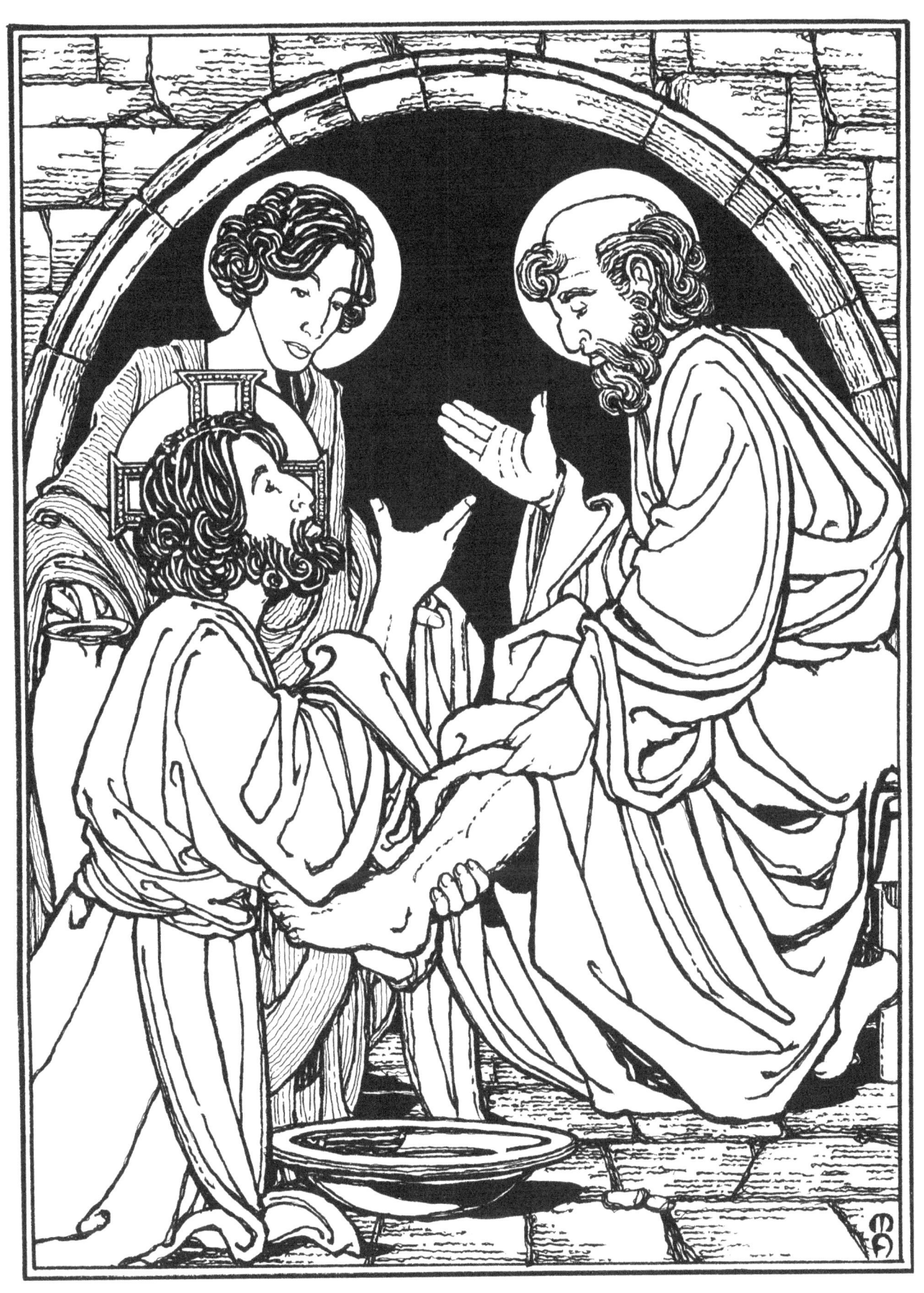

The Washing of the Feet

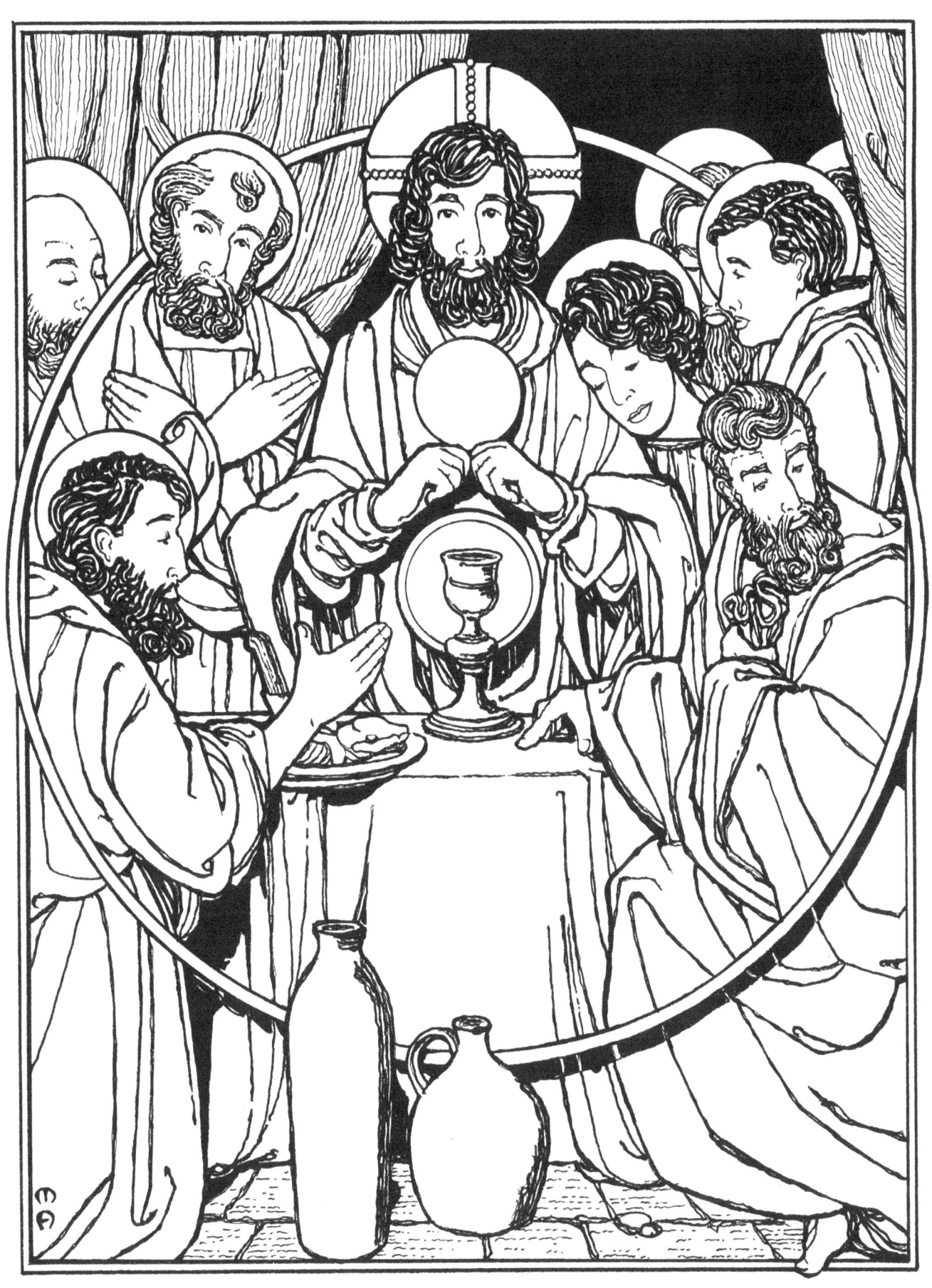

The Institution of the Eucharist

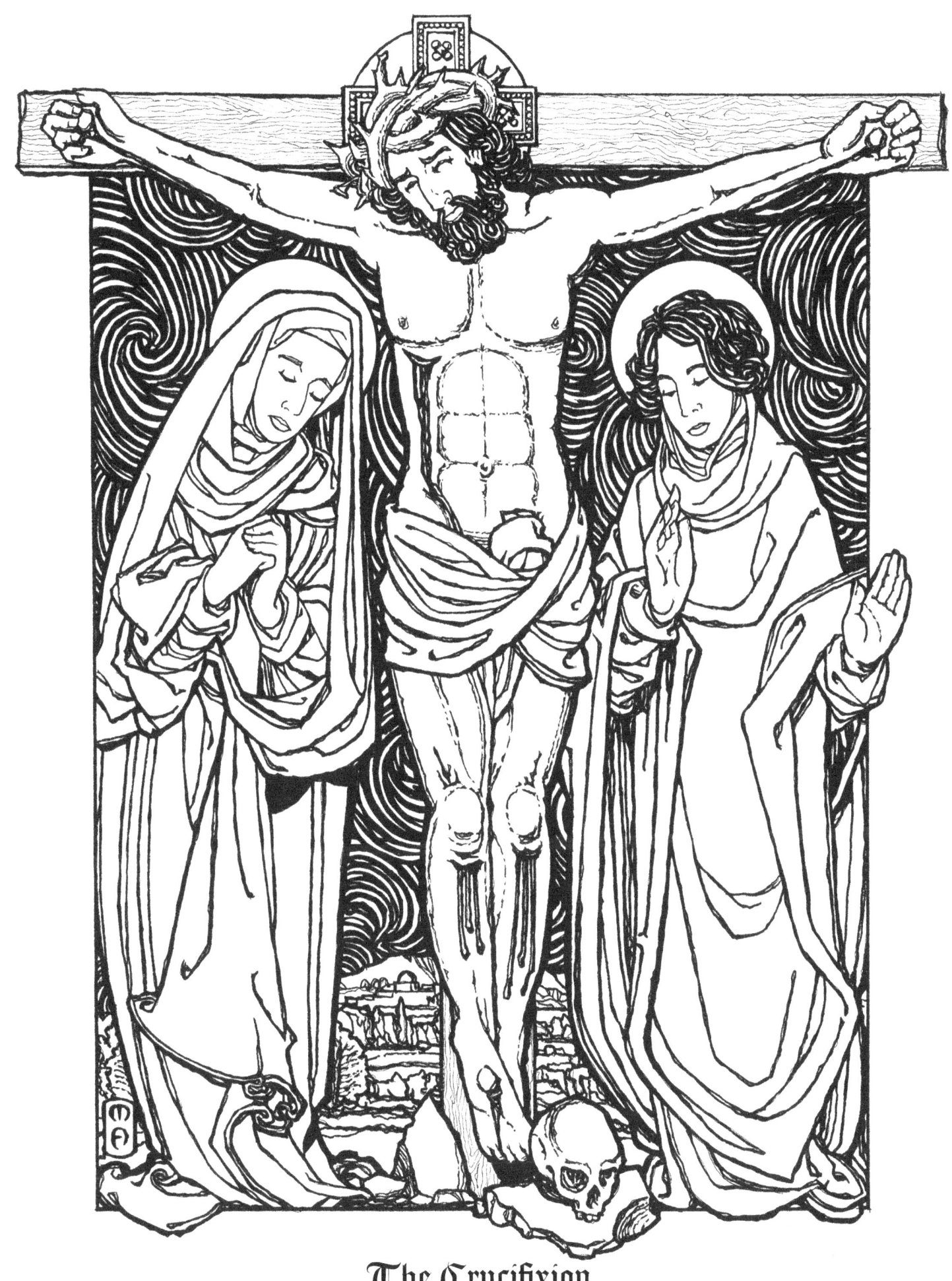

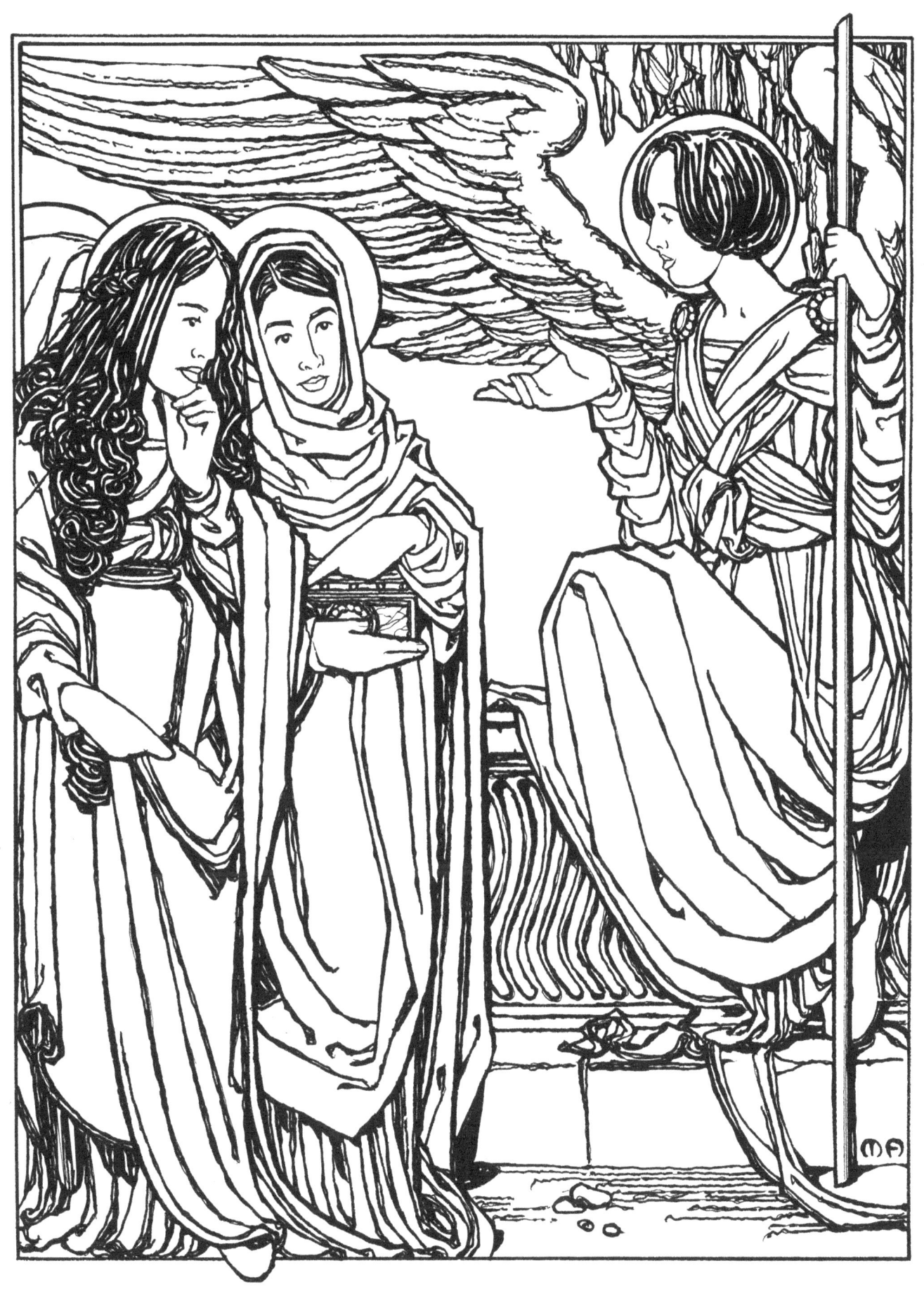

The Women at the Tomb

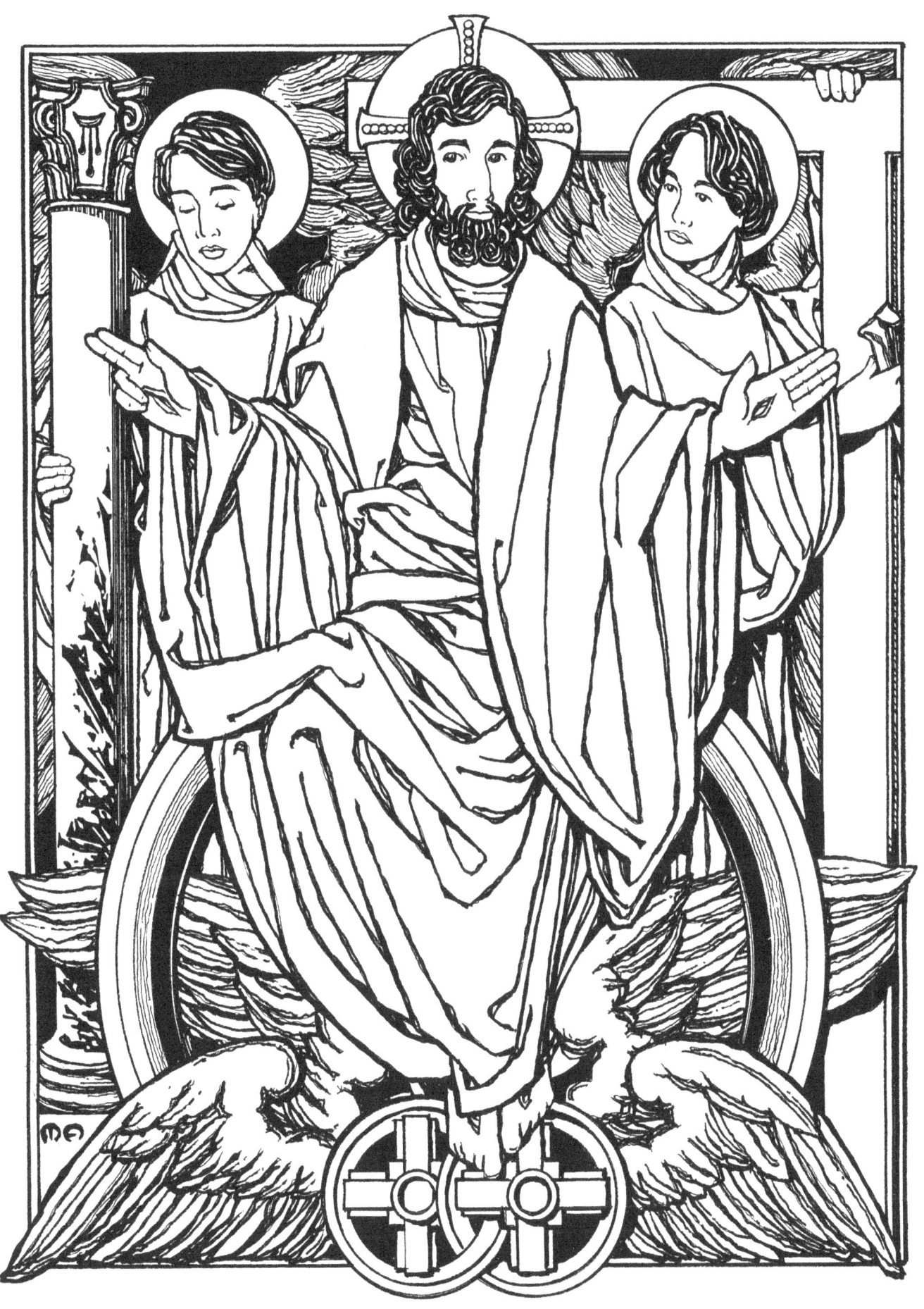

The Resurrection

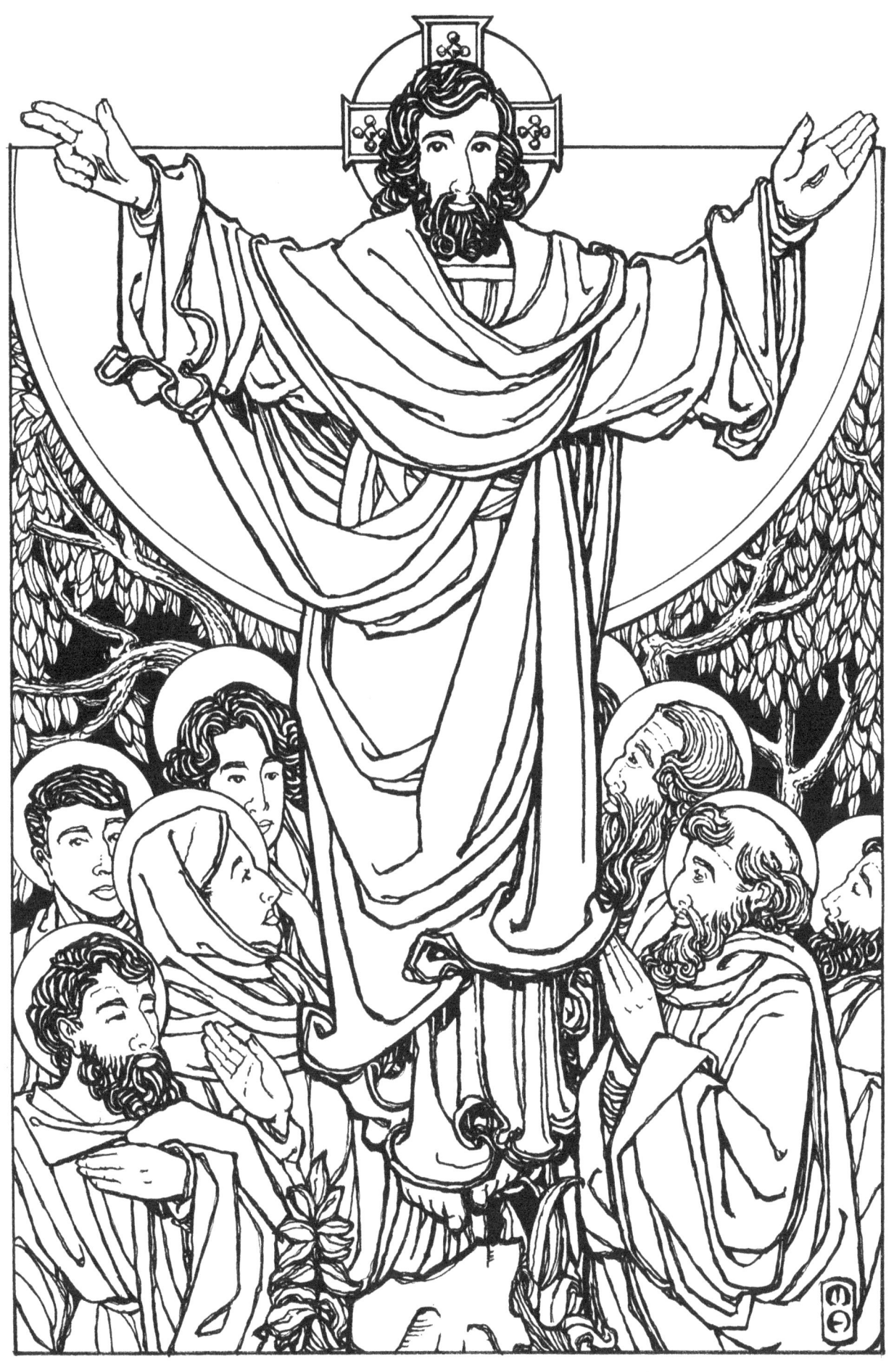

The Ascension

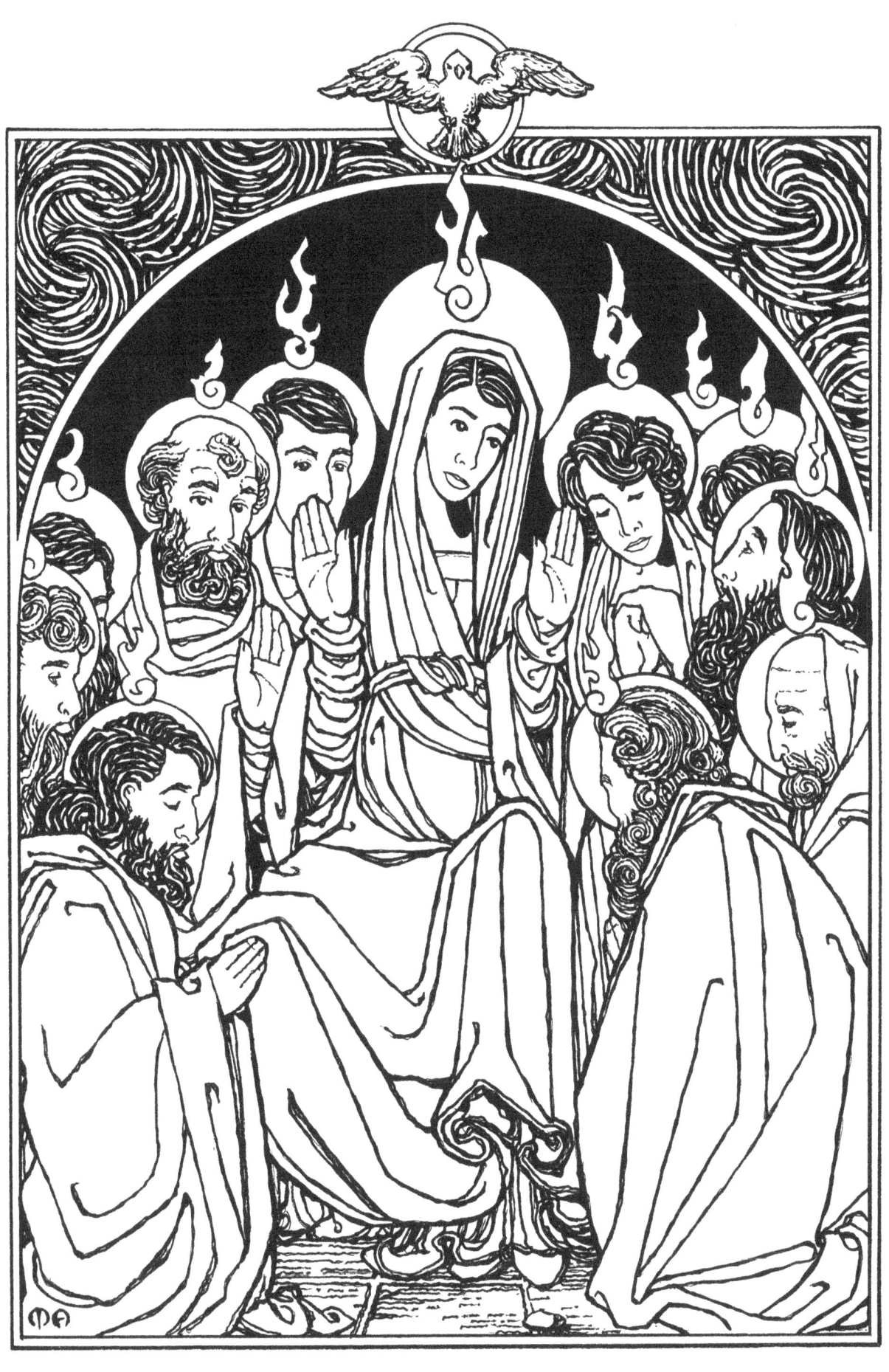

Pentecost

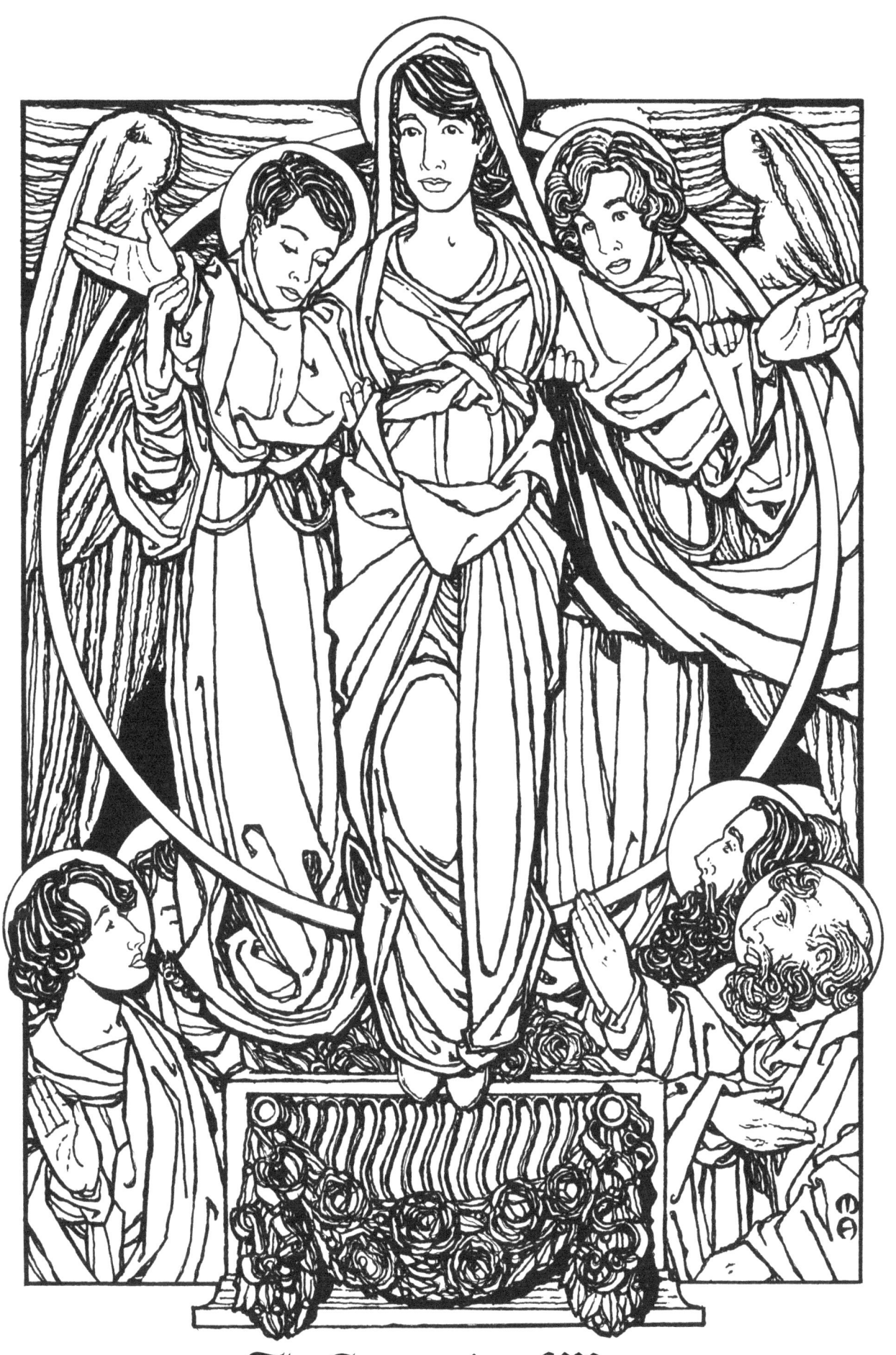

The Assumption of Mary

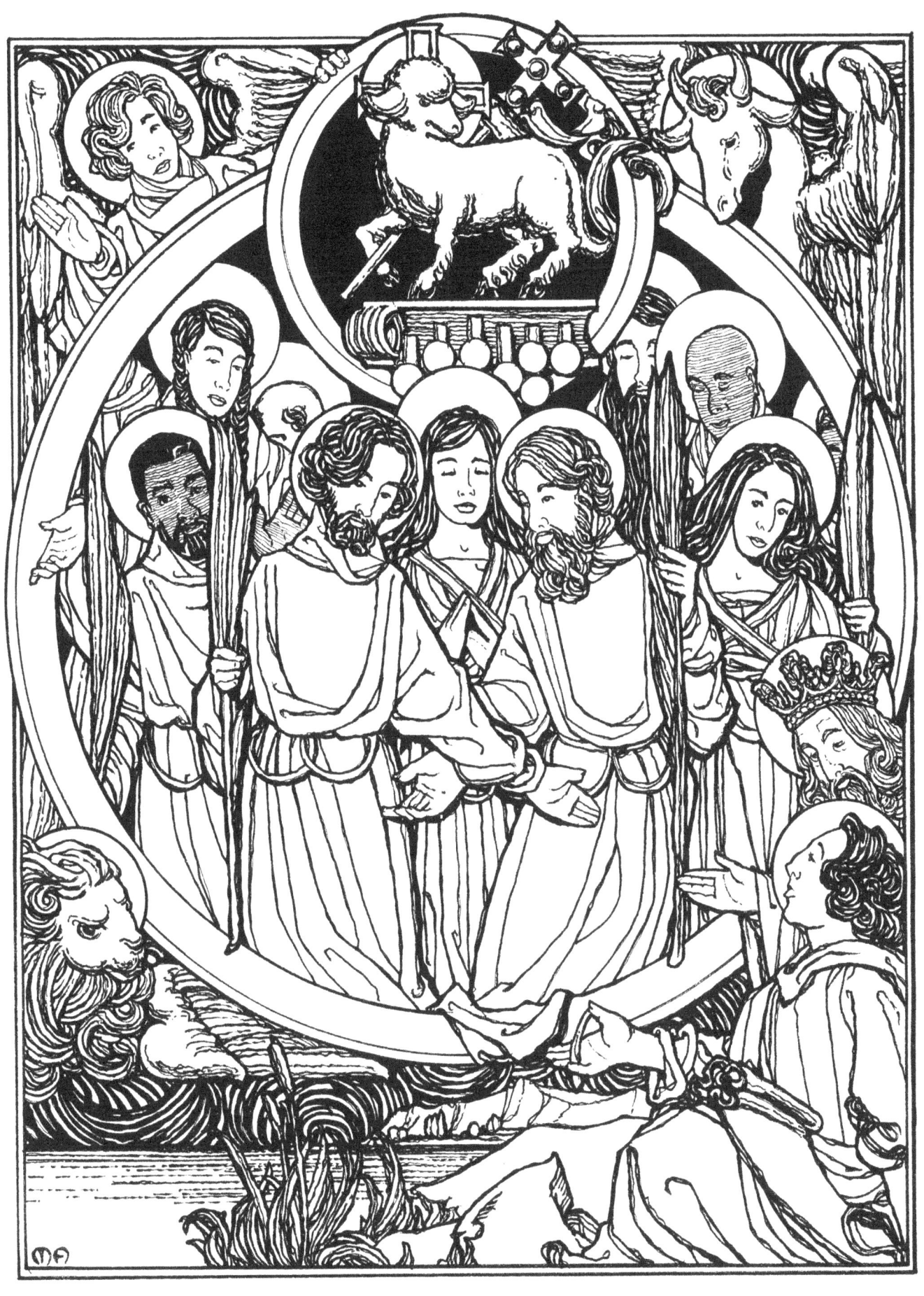

The Feast of All Saints

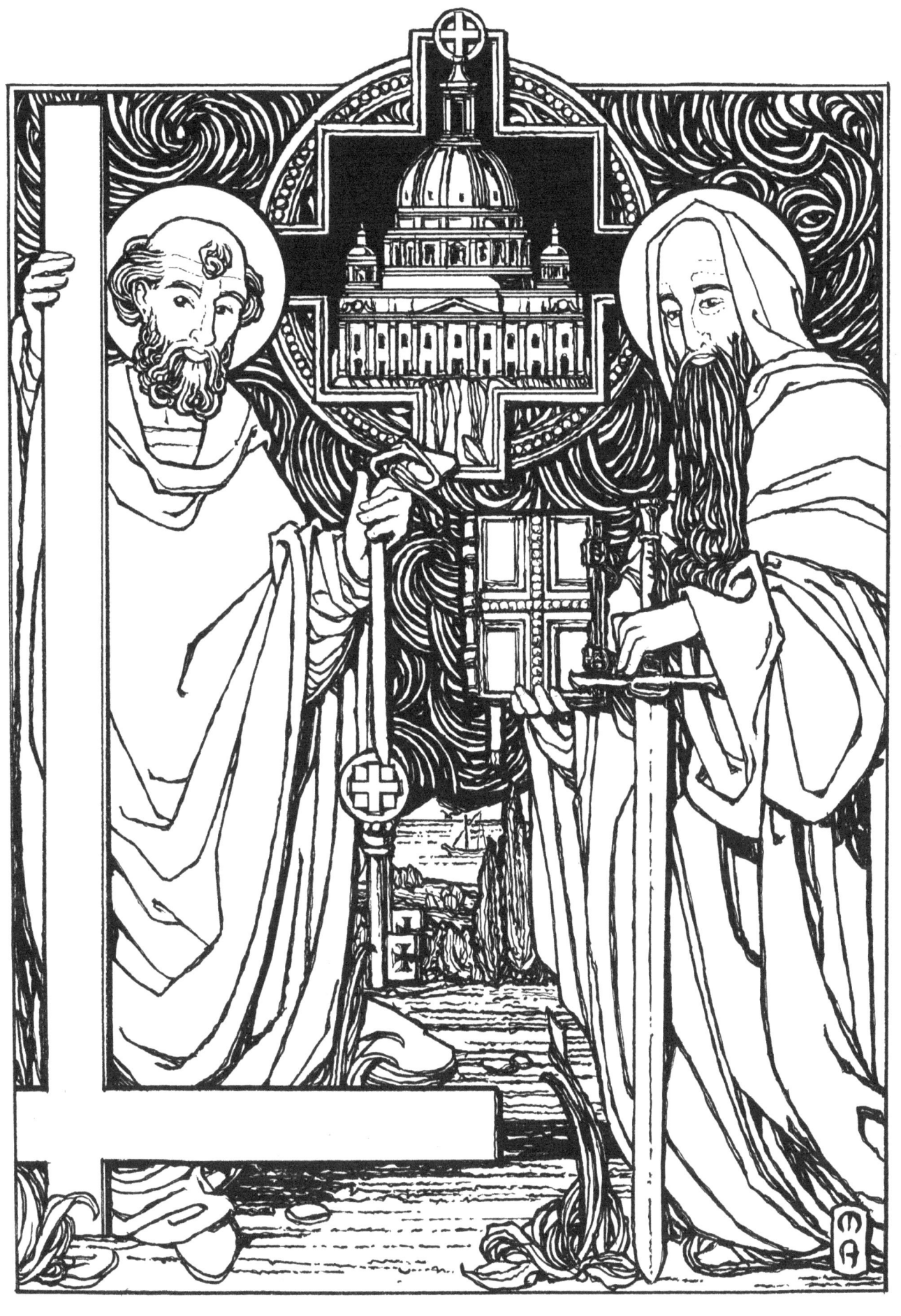
Saints Peter and Paul

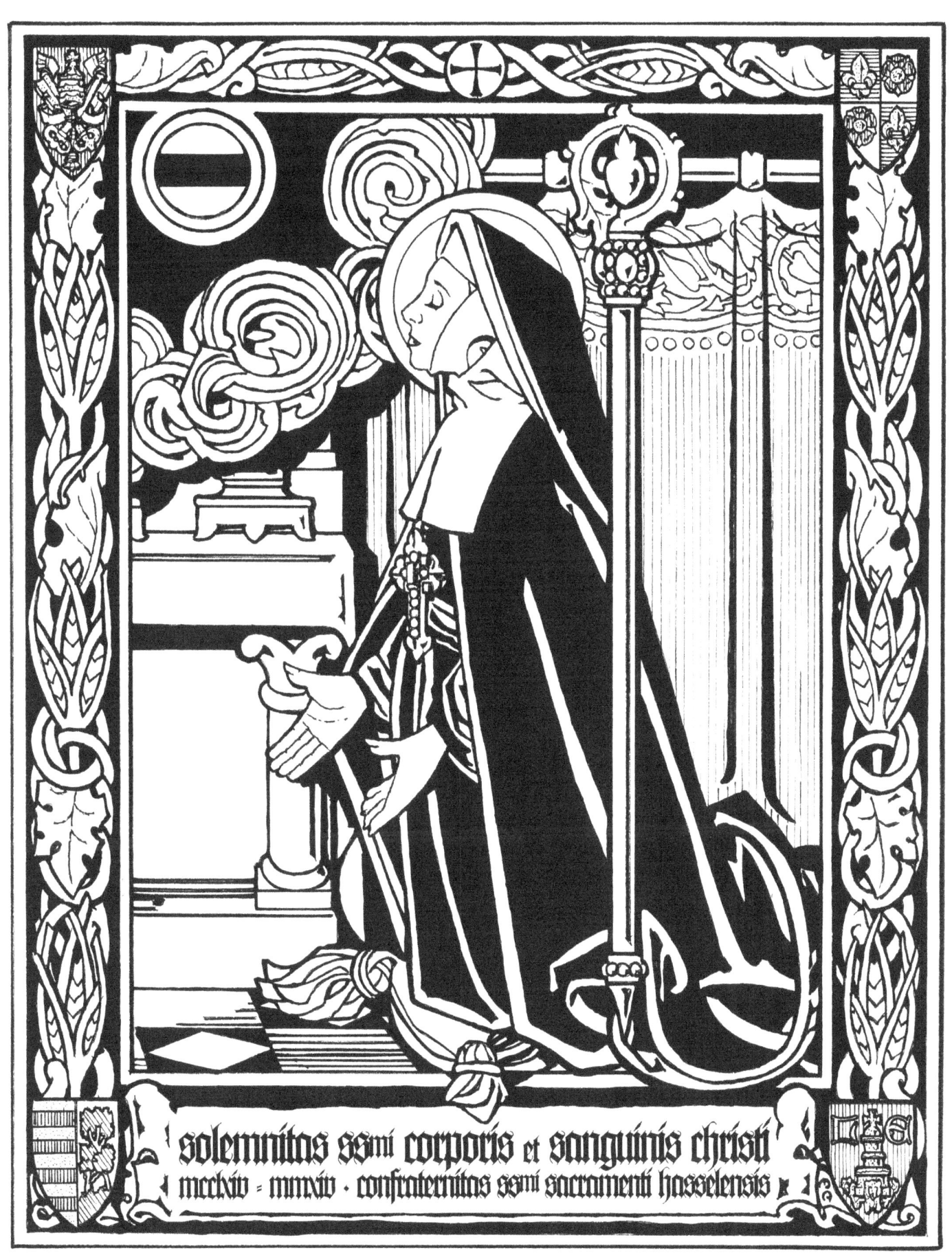

The Feast of Corpus Christi

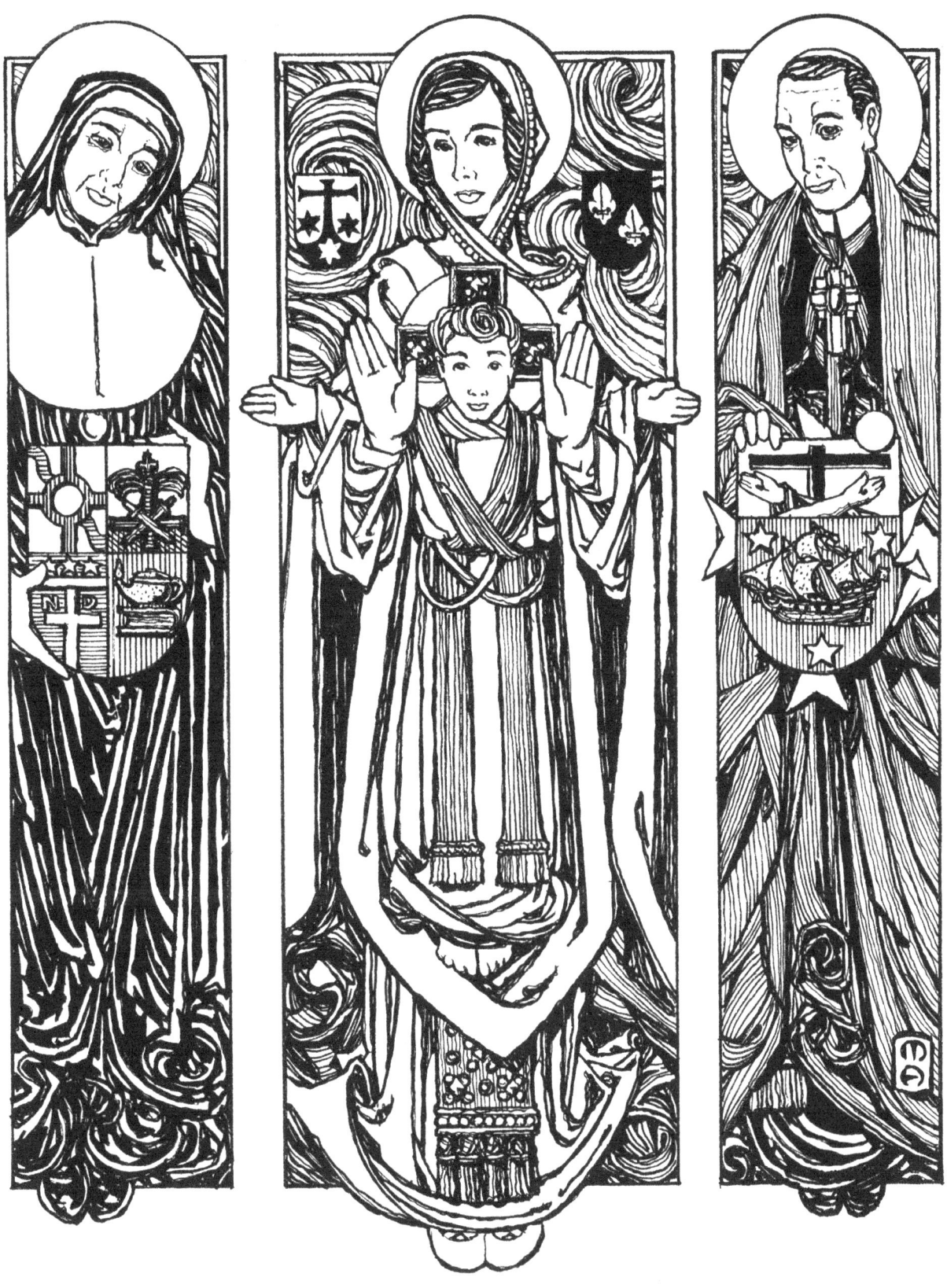

Titles of Our Lady

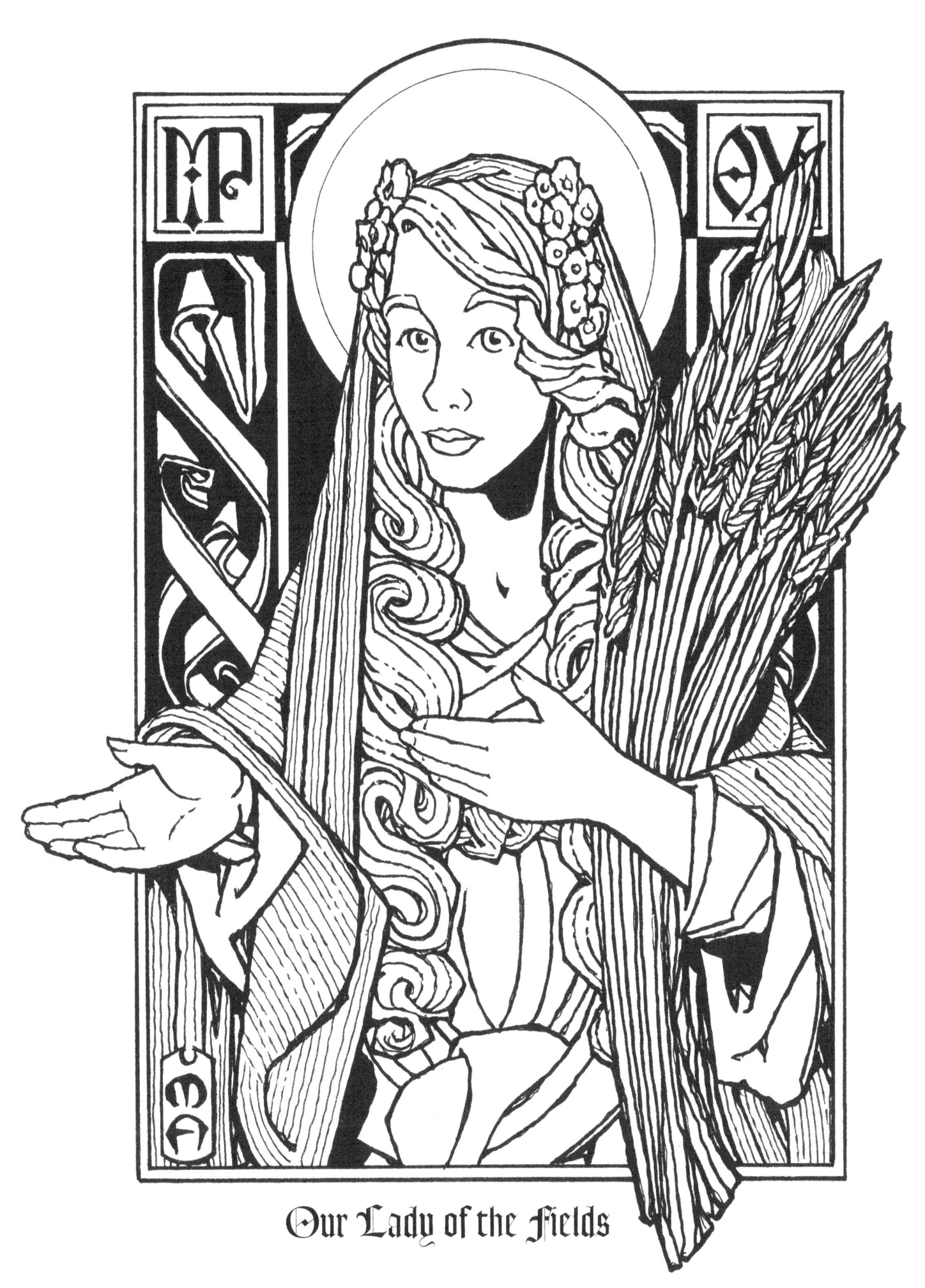

Our Lady of the Fields

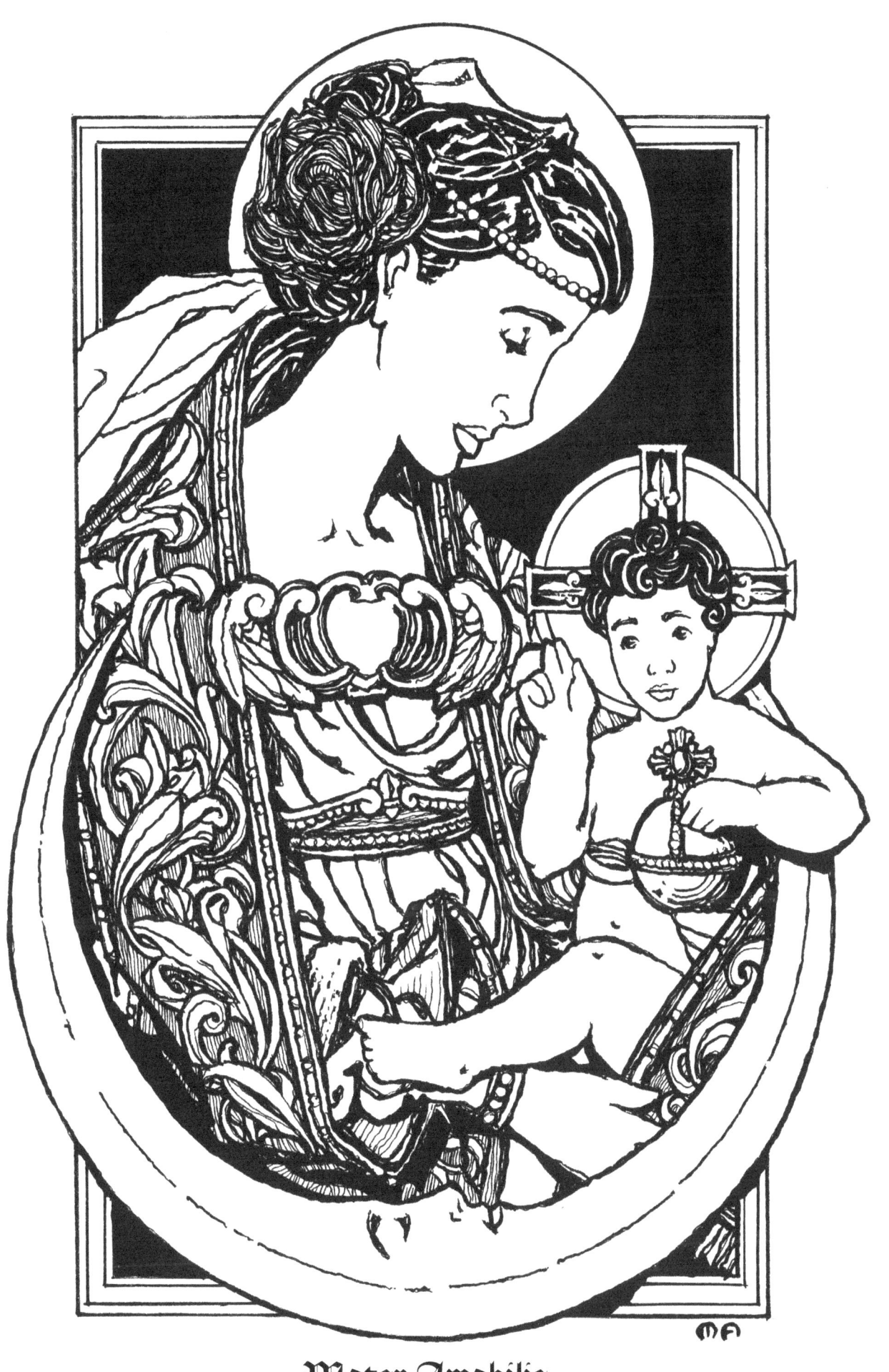

Mater Amabilis

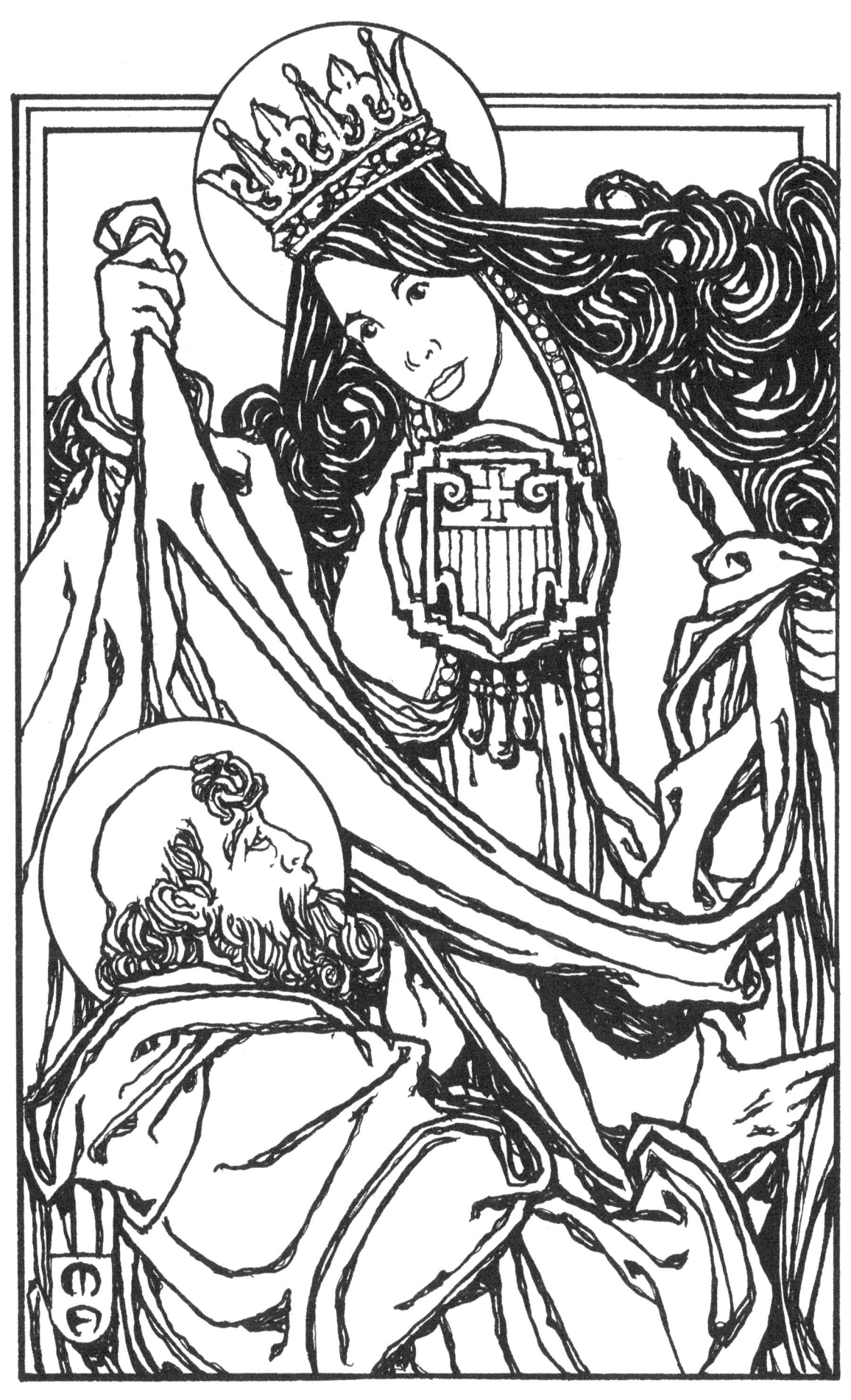

Our Lady of Ransom

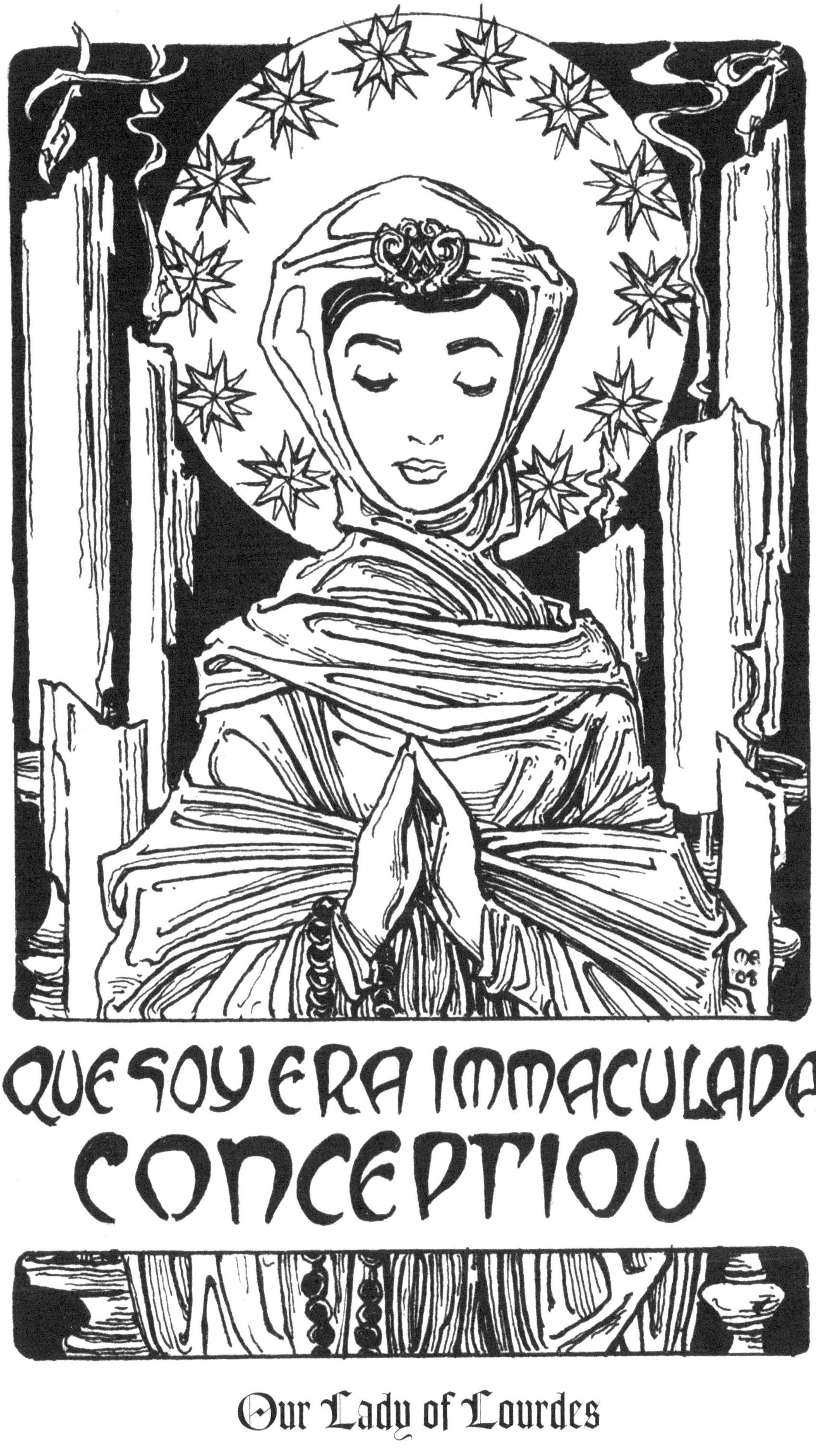

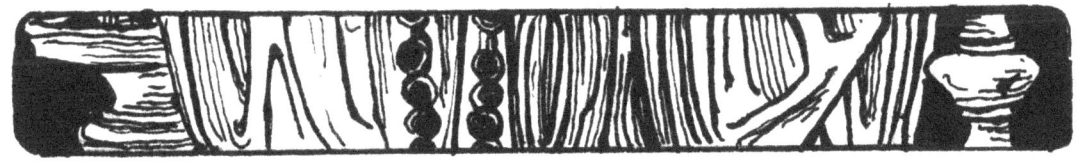

Our Lady of Lourdes

www.ingramcontent.com/pod-product-compliance
Lightning Source LLC
Chambersburg PA
CBHW040544220526
45473CB00016B/3018